Starting out with (

Contents

Introduction 2
History 2
Components of a Quadcopter 7
    Chassis 8
    Control Board 8
    GPS receiver 9
    Motors 9
    Electronic Speed Control (ESC) 10
    Radio Receiver 10
    Transmitter 10
    Battery 11
Choosing a first Quadcopter 12
Commonly Available Ready to Fly Quadcopters 13
    DJi: 13
    Blade: 15
    Walkera 17
Where to Buy From 18
Learning to fly: 19
    Batteries 19
The Legal Bit... 20
First Flight 22
Crash!! 25

Next Steps 27
Photography and FPV 27
Reality Check 27
FPV: 29
Aerial Photography 30
Gimbals 31
GoPro Cameras 32
General Filming Tips 34
Filming Accidents, Emergencies and Disasters 37
Conclusion 38
About the Author: 39

Introduction

In the past 12 months, there has been an explosion of interest in flying outdoor sized quadcopter and other multi-rotor machines – driven by the introduction of a number of excellent ready to fly aircraft and the diminishing cost of parts and kits for DIY builders as well.

The majority of information available is aimed at the American market, where the hobby is slightly more mature and the opportunities for flying somewhat greater, and also for the DIY community, where kits and individual components are readily available to construct a good quality aircraft – provided you have the skills! This book is therefore aimed at the UK hobby flyer and concentrates predominantly on the ready to fly (RTF) machines available in the 1.5-2.5Kg medium lift category.

History

Model Electric Helicopters were very much late to the party in terms of model aviation and to a certain extent, are still seen as something of a toy by some of the serious model aircraft community. No doubt this is part due to the fact that they are cheaper to purchase, easier to fly and generally more crash resistant. Land a balsa wood and IC engine fixed wing aircraft a little heavily and the chances are that your afternoons flying is over, while a small electric helicopter can drop 20' out of the air and sustain minimal damage, often requiring little more than a wipe down of the canopy and a fresh battery to be up in the air again.

The main driver behind electric powered flight – both fixed wing and rotary is without doubt the development of cheap and powerful Lithium Ion battery technology coupled with high output, high efficiency electric motors. This allows very high energy densities and high power at a very low weight, making electric aircraft a viable proposition. Prior to this, some flyers had experimented with NiCad and NiMH batteries and a limited number of models had been produced, but flight times were short and the flight envelopes quite limited.

The second major development was linked to the humble mobile phone, where the mass production of miniaturised GPS, solid state gyros and accelerometers – used to orientate the screen when the phone is turned, meant that a complete set of flight electronics could be put together for a much reduced cost.

Early multi-rotor helicopters used standard model aircraft solid state gyros – often 3,4 or 6 of them working together in different axis to stabilise the model, but the pilot still need to correct for altitude and wind. Smaller craft still utilise this technology, as it can be squeezed into a flier weighing no more than 20 grams.

Led initially by the DIY market – where development boards capable of interfacing with accelerometers harvested from Nintendo Wii remotes along with mini-GPS packages, proved that a small, lightweight computerised control unit could be constructed and that could maintain an aircraft's position and altitude to within a few metres whatever the weather conditions – and for just a few hundred pounds. Open source software gave experimenters the ability to tweak the parameters of the aircraft to suit different payloads and motor configurations.

Parallel development in the professional UAV (Unmanned Aerial Vehicle) market had led to more powerful command and control systems aimed at drones and aerial photography platforms. Based on similar technologies, it was now possible to purchase a multi-rotor machine, complete with a PC based ground station, capable of autonomous flight for a few tens of thousands of pounds.

It was clear therefore, that a gap in the market for a mid-sized, cost effective, computer controlled multi-rotor helicopter in ready to fly format existed and many major companies rushed to bring their products to market. Arguably first there was the Parrot AR Drone. Although seen by many as a toy – not least in part due to the use of WiFi and a smart phone to control, the aircraft is still a complex flying machine, capable of unaided stable flight in calmer conditions. This was soon followed by the DJi Phantom, Blade 350QX and the very similar Walkera QR-X350. All these aircraft feature GPS, computerised control and a degree of autonomous flight and all are designed to have cameras mounted to them. Costs range from £250 or so for a basic "Bind and Fly" 'copter requiring a transmitter to complete, up to around £1100 for a full featured camera equipped platform, ready to fly straight out of the box.

Another aspect has been the development of lightweight, high quality camera systems. A range of very lightweight cameras – from 20 grams or so upwards had been developed for model aircraft, but these suffered from fairly limited image quality, usually being standard definition only and could be quite fragile if the aircraft crash landed. Action cameras designed for skiers and mountain bikers however are designed to be much more robust, often housed in waterproof mounts with polycarbonate casing. The most popular has been the GoPro series – now in Series 3+ guise, which can take stills up to 12Mp and video up to 2.7K (Beyond HD) resolution. Medium lift multi-rotors can carry a GoPro with ease, even along with a stabilising gimbal. (More about this later)

Components of a Quadcopter

To properly fly a quadcopter, it is important to understand a little about what makes it lift off the ground and remain controllable. In order to make something fly, you need to create Lift. This is done by creating a low pressure area of air over a wing or rotor, so that the aircraft is "sucked" upwards. In a fixed wing aircraft, the air passing over the top shape of the wing is sped up, thus creating the low pressure and in fact in helicopters and multi-rotors, the science is very similar. Conventional helicopters use one blade to create the lift, while a second tail rotor balances the rotational forces of the main rotor and also provides the ability to turn. Forward, back and side motion is created by tilting the rotor blades as they rotate, thus tipping the helicopter slightly and altering the direction of thrust from the main rotor.

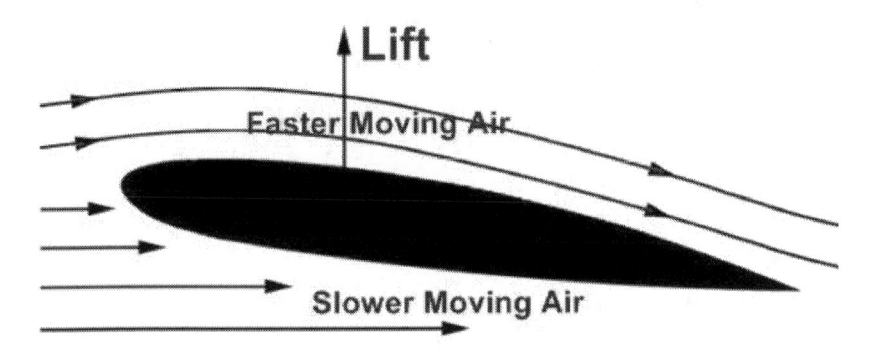

Lift
Faster Moving Air
Slower Moving Air

In a multi-rotor helicopter, things are slightly different. 3, 4 or more spinning propellers mounted vertically provide the lift, but these generally have a fixed "pitch" and cannot be tilted to provide thrust in another direction. Instead, the speed of each propeller is varied, thus causing the whole helicopter to tilt, providing directional control. Each propeller therefore has its own electric motor and electronic speed control (ESC) and the electronics to translate the control instructions from the pilot into the correct motor responses, taking into account the aircraft's altitude, attitude and other factors. For this reason, all multi-copters are essentially "Fly by Wire" and cannot be referenced back to any conventional flying machine – although it could be argued the "Flying Bedstead" used to train Apollo astronauts comes fairly close!

The component parts are therefore as follows:

Chassis

4 arms (In the case of a quadcopter) plus space for electronics, battery and payload. Generally a robust frame that can absorb crash landing impacts, but also provide a stable platform for cameras and other equipment.

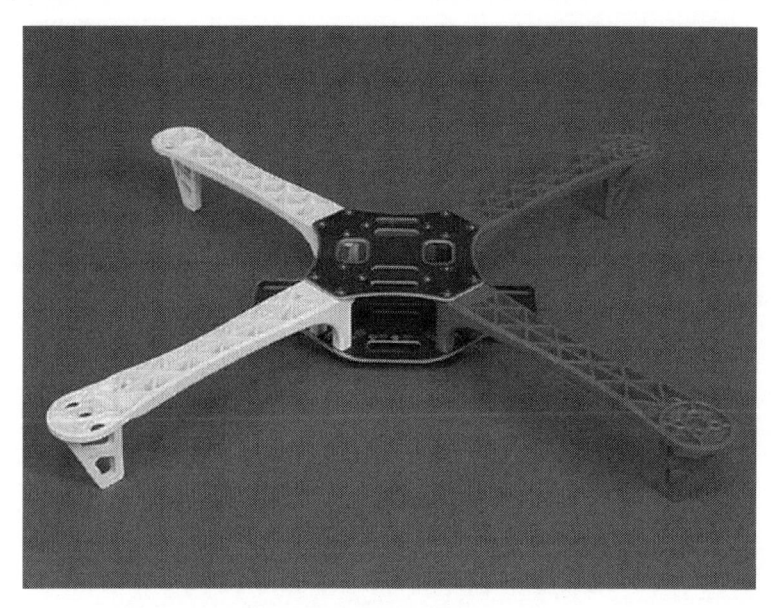

Control Board
The brains of the system. Receiving control signals from the radio control system, GPS, compass, altimeter, accelerometers and other sensors, the control board calculates the precise speed each motor requires to carry out the control instruction and monitors the outcome, providing additional and continuous corrections. The controller may well have a degree of autonomy and be programmed to fly to a "Home" GPS location in the event of transmitter signal failure.

GPS receiver
Usually a separate board, this receives signals from the American GPS satellite network and pinpoints the current location of the helicopter to within a few metres. This allows "Return to Home", "Position Hold" and other features to operate correctly.

Motors
1 per propeller, mounted at the end of each arm. Early designs used a gearbox to decrease rotor speed and increase torque, but modern, high speed, high torque brushless motors will generally directly drive the propellers. Brushless motors are designed whereby the coils that produce the magnetic force remain stationary and the shaft is connected to

permanent magnets. The benefits of this sort of motor is that it has fewer moving parts – no brushes or commutator to wear out, but the flip side is that a special controller is needed to provide the carefully monitored Alternating Current required to drive the motor.

Electronic Speed Control (ESC)

This takes the output from the control board and increases the current, frequency and voltage to that required by the motor. The board will also monitor the motor for short circuits or overcurrent, so that if the helicopter crash lands, the motors will be stopped, thus avoiding any further damage.

Radio Receiver

Most modern quadcopters use 2.4GHz frequency radio control systems, but a few may be shipped with 5.8GHz to avoid interference from wifi based camera systems while older 35MHz model aircraft sets can still be found. In any case, the receiver will decode the commands from the receiver into 4 or more channels of information and feed this to the control board. There are a limited number of channels available in the 35MHz band, while 2.4GHz has a much higher capacity, with the radio control systems switching frequencies to avoid interference. 5.8GHz also restricts control range to about 400m, due to the propagation of radio waves at this frequency, with only DJi currently shipping transmitters of this type and even then, only where a WiFI camera is fitted as standard (FC40, Vision and Vision+)

Transmitter

This will be paired, or bound to the receiver and is probably the most customisable aspect of a ready to fly quadcopter. The basic design calls for 2 control sticks, both of which can move in 2 axis –left and right and up and down. The UK normally uses "Mode 2", which means that the left stick controls altitude – by moving the stick up and down to increase and decrease power, and yaw (Turning) by moving the stick left and right. The right stick controls forward (Pitch) and side movement (Roll) in the same way.

Added to this may be other switches – to control advanced features like Return to Home, rates, which alter the sensitivity of the gyros, allowing for more aerobatic flying and also control additional features like a camera or retractable undercarriage. On advanced transmitters, it is possible to alter the "slope" of a control stick, so that the operation may be set to non-linear. This might allow for the power to be delivered more progressively or for yaw to be more precisely controlled. It may also incorporate additional sticks or knobs to alter the angle of the camera with respect to the helicopter.

It used to be standard practice to fit rechargeable batteries to the transmitter, but modern designs use far less energy and are not designed for the slightly lower voltage that NiCad or NiMH batteries output. A set of high capacity alkaline batteries will last weeks or months in any case.

The advantage of 2.4GHz & 5.8GHz systems is that it is very difficult for the signal to be intercepted by another radio control transmitter and control lost. The transmitter and receiver are bound or locked together, so even an identical transmitter on the same frequency cannot take over control.

Battery

The Lithium Polymer - LiPo battery will usually be the heaviest single item on the quadcopter, but its size and weight will determine the flight time and to a certain extent, the dynamics of the flight envelope. While early machines struggled to stay airborne for more than a few minutes, the latest designs have flight durations approaching 30 minutes. More than enough time to fly a round trip of 10 miles or more!

Batteries are rated in 3 ways. The "S" number relates to the number of individual battery cells used to make up the complete battery. Each cell is rated at 3.7V – due to the chemistry of the battery, so a typical 3S (3 cell) battery will have a voltage of 11.1V. The second rating is the power output, expressed as mA/hour. This is the maximum current the battery can deliver for an hour before it is discharged. A typical battery could be 1200 – 2800mA/Hour, but the new Phantom2 battery is closer to 5200mA/Hour, hence the extended flight time. The 3rd rating is the C or charge rating. The higher the number, the faster the battery can be charged. Most batteries will be at least 15C these days. Chargers will have settings allowing you to set the correct charge level, while older batteries may benefit from a slower – lower C charge.

Batteries should be stored 75% charged and never left flat for any length of time.

Follow the safety warnings carefully, as these batteries contain lithium, which reacts with air, causing massive heat build up and quite often a chemical fire. If the casing becomes swollen or damaged, follow the battery safety information in the flight section later in this book.

Other equipment may include cameras, video links and telemetry systems, but we will cover these later.

Choosing a first Quadcopter

The first decision has to be what is the purpose of buying a quadcopter? If you are simply after an easy to learn helicopter, then you may find that some designs offer too little in terms of aerobatic capability, are not challenging enough to fly and you may all too soon become bored of them. For many, the attraction is that a quadcopter makes for a stable and easy to fly camera platform, either for aerial photography or as a First Person View (FPV) aircraft, where you fly from a pilots' eye view while remaining firmly glued to the ground.

The good news is that some of the designs have different modes, allowing you to fly in a lightweight acrobatic format one day and as a fully loaded FPV camera platform the next, with the dynamic capabilities of the model adapted to suit the task in hand. Even if your final goal is aerial photography, it is still advisable to get a good few flying hours under your belt without the cameras attached, as the cost of the video equipment is likely to be more than the cost of the helicopter, so any crashes while learning will be correspondingly more expensive!

Whatever you decide to get, a flight simulator and possibly a small "lounge" flyer are an excellent investment. Phoenix R/C now offer their version 5 R/C simulator with both the DJi Phantom and Blade 350QX models included. Crashing repeatedly in the virtual world might make you think twice about attempting advanced aerobatics when taking your new flier out for the first time and whizzing a micro 'copter around indoors will make the controls much more familiar as well. Many of the crash videos you see on YouTube and Vimeo are first and second flights, where inexperienced pilots have flown beyond their ability level, leading to expensive mistakes.

Small quadcopters – EG: Hubsan X4, with just gyro stabilisation are a totally different machine to fly, being much more skittish and difficult to control. They are not really suitable for flying outside, unless it is a very calm day, but as the propellers are exposed and rotate at high speed, be careful flying near other people, indoors or out.

Commonly Available Ready to Fly Quadcopters

Concentrating on the 3 main manufacturers of medium lift, sub 3.5Kg quadcopters available in the UK, we have the following observations to make on the various models available. These are not recommendations or reviews, just our experience of the various machines. We have not included the Parrot AR, as this is not really designed for outdoor flying at any distance, as control is only via WiFi and the payload is insufficient for all but the smallest camera. Their latest system may be something of a game changer, with a dual joystick controller and wifi booster, but early indications are that it is not really in the same league as the aircraft below, with stability and control issues making flying it quite a challenge.

DJi:

DJ Innovations are a Chinese company with a history in professional heavy lift designs and also a range of flight electronics, including the well respected NAZA and WooKong range of controllers, GPS modules, ground stations, camera gimbals and radio links. Their first consumer product was the crossover Flame Wheel series, which includes the relatively cheap F350 & 450 quadcopter chassis. Although not sold by DJi as ready to fly, a large number of model aircraft shops build these up to order and bundle them with a suitable radio control system.

DJi's first ready to fly quadcopter was the Phantom, and this remains in production, along with the Phantom2 and also a range of camera equipped machines at increasing prices. The original Phantom has a flight time of around 7 – 12 minutes and was designed to carry a GoPro Hero camera in a static mount. DJi then added a lightweight gimbal – called the Zenmuse H3-2D to the range, which added professional levels of camera stability to the system and turned the Phantom into the hobby aerial platform of choice for many.

Recognising the short battery time – particularly when carrying a gimbal and camera, the Phantom2 is an updated design, with a different body shell incorporating a much larger "smart" battery and better off the shelf gimbal and FPV support through ready fitted wiring. Cashing in on the aerial photography boom, DJi now offer two Phantom2 variants with built in cameras. The Vision features an HD camera mounted to a simple tilting mount, while the Vision+ has a full 3D, 3 axis gimbal and an HD camera capable of up to 60 frames per second for slow motion recording. A cheaper FC 40 model is based upon the original Phantom and has a fixed lower definition camera.

All are widely regarded as easy to fly and crash resistant, but the facility to customise is quite limited, due to the enclosed body shell and proprietary radio control system. The CANBUS system allows extra DJi modules, including a video overlay of flight data onto a video link to be added, but 3rd party support is minimal, limited to aftermarket landing gear and prop guards, plus batteries for the original Phantom. The radio control system is considered quite basic and the transmission range is sometimes questionable on the 5.8GHz sets, with some owners upgrading to different systems. The latest firmware for the control systems on the Phantom2 series restricts flying in controlled airspace around airports and also allows flight ceilings and distance from the operator to be set as well.

DJi also market a ground control system, allowing you to set waypoints and heights, effectively programming your Phantom quadcopter for autonomous flight. A fully featured PC based professional version is available for a significant investment, or a free iPad app contains some of the features and requiring just an additional data module to be fitted to the quadcopter and plugged into the Naza control system. The CAA has stated it is happy for pilots to use these waypoint systems, subject to them maintaining visual contact with the aircraft at all times. This limits their usefulness in the UK, but they are proving popular overseas, where flights of 5 miles or more are now being successfully completed and documented.

Blade:
Blade have a long history in designing and selling a wide range of helicopters, mainly conventional single rotor fixed pitch (FP) and collective pitch (CP) aerobatic designs. Their first medium lift quadcopter – the 350QX is a direct competitor to the DJi Phantom, but is designed more with model aircraft hobby fliers in mind. The main feature missing on the Phantom is the ability to switch to an advanced acrobatic setting, called Agility mode. This allows flips and rolls to be performed, as well as increasing the maximum speed of the quadcopter. The controller also allows for a beginners mode – called Smart, which turns the 350QX into a stable camera platform which will also avoid collisions with the operator thanks to GPS positioning that establishes a safe zone in which the operator and any spectators should stand. This makes the helicopter more suitable for flying in back gardens and restricted spaces, where lower altitudes and closer proximity to the operator might be encountered. A third, Stability mode allows for GPS locked hovering, with additional altitude sensors to keep the helicopter locked to a spot; perfect for aerial photography.

Flight time is comparable to the original Phantom – about 7-10 minutes, as is cost, but the offer of a Bind and Fly version makes it a cheaper purchase for owners of other Blade helicopters with compatible 5 channel or more radio controls, such as the Spectrum DX5i.

On the down side, original models had problems with blades breaking mid-flight and this is still reported as a problem even with the re-designed propellers, with blade strikes onto the bodywork causing premature failure and some quite hard crashes. After market kits that raise the propellers 10mm or so do seem to help cure this problem. A gimbal can be added, but this needs to be sourced from aftermarket suppliers.

There have also been serious issues around flyaways (Where the quadcopter loses its positional and heading information and proceeds to fly away from the operator who may be left with little or no control), with the version 2 software addressing what is seen as a design issue with the in-built compass and GPS unit. Although similar issues have been flagged up with all the designs mentioned here, there does seem to be a particular problem with this design. We have not experienced the issue ourselves, but always ensure the helicopter has full lock before we fly and we also avoid changing modes while airborne – something which it is reported can cause the failure.

Walkera

Another company with its roots in conventional helicopters, their QR X350 is probably the most futuristic looking of the three, but the hardest to find in the UK! Available either as an FPV – with the video receiver and monitor built into the radio control unit but requiring the addition of a GoPro, and as a basic version without a receiver for those wanting to add their own, the helicopter features the same flight modes as the Phantom, as well as a similar range of add ons, including telemetry and video transmission. A gimbal is available directly from the manufacturer for those wanting to mount a compensated camera.

This quadcopter is aimed at the beginner, lacking the Agility mode of the Blade, but can be bought quite cheaply compared to the Phantom. Flying is very similar to the Phantom, but confusingly, the LED indicators are reversed, so green is forward – as opposed to red for the Phantom! Just be careful if you get to fly both...

Where to Buy From

All these helicopters can be bought online from a variety of retailers, but we urge you to buy from a UK based first tier dealer, as the support will be much better. They can also advise and often fit prior to delivery any add on modules and also test fly the aircraft, so you know it is ready to go as soon as you receive it.

Buying from grey importers could lead to warranty issues and also a total lack of support if and when you have a crash or two. None of the manufacturers have a direct UK presence, so you are reliant on their tier one dealers for warranty repairs and support.

Now comes the problem. Some helicopter and model aircraft shops are still quite "sniffy" about quadcopters, considering them to be mere toys and not serious model aircraft. Please therefore be a little cautious when visiting these shops as you may end up leaving with a very different view of the hobby and clutching a very expensive and difficult to fly single rotor! As fliers of single rotor CP electric helicopters ourselves, we can tell you that the learning curve is much steeper and the results for FPV and aerial photography much poorer. Even the national associations – let alone the local clubs are not really geared up to multi-rotor yet, with limited support and not a lot of interest. The DIY multi rotor fraternity is a little friendlier, but it is a small and quite closeted group, with limited trade support. This makes ready to fly Quadcopters almost a hobby by itself, so you may have to end up buying from an online specialist retailer some distance away from you. Thank God for the internet and 24 hour couriers!

The good news is that things are changing and at club and national level there is growing acceptance and understanding of the market for these machines. Even the "serious" radio control magazines now carry articles and reviews of the quadcopters, as well as adverts from specialist suppliers.

Learning to fly:

So hopefully by now you have ordered your new Quadcopter and the postman delivered an exciting box to your doorstep. Before you rush off to the local park, let's cover some basics first.

Batteries

Lithium Polymer batteries can be dangerous. They can overheat if damaged and spontaneously combust! Basic safety rules are printed on the battery and must be followed.

- Never charge a damaged battery. If it is swollen or the casing damaged, put it in a bucket of salt water and leave it for 48 hours. You can then dispose of it at a local waste site. Do not put in with household waste or general recycling. Some retailers have battery recycling bins that will accept LiPo batteries.
- Always use the correct charger. Ordinary NiCad battery chargers WILL damage a Lithium battery.
- Always charge on a non-flammable surface and NEVER in the helicopter. We use an old paving slab in the garage. Therefore, if the battery does have an issue, it is unlikely to cause any damage.
- Never fully discharge a Lithium battery, as it will never recover. As soon as the battery warning lights come on, or the helicopter starts to lose height, land immediately.
- Never charge a hot or warm battery. Let it cool down first.
- Batteries can be charged up to about 100 times, sometimes a lot less. Don't risk an old battery, as it might let you down at the worst possible moment.

The Legal Bit...

The Civil Aviation Authority Air Navigation Order has a few things to say about flying model aircraft, but until you strap a camera onto it, it basically boils down to this:

- You must have permission of the landowner for your take off site.
- You must not endanger any other person at any time
- You must not fly out of visual range
- You must not fly above 400'
- You must not fly in restricted airspace. This includes military sites, airports and royal palaces.
- You must not fly for commercial purposes unless qualified and insured to do so.

We suggest you download the important bits and read them thoroughly. More info can be found here: http://www.fpvuk.org/fpv-law/ as well as a link to the ANO itself on the CAA website.

We would also suggest you get some 3rd party liability insurance, just in case the worst does happen and you flatten somebody.
http://www.fpvuk.org/become-a-member/ Join the FPV organisation and you get £5M PLI thrown in. BMFA also offer a similar scheme, but it costs a little more and there is less association support for quadcopters from them at the moment.
http://www.bmfa.org/Membership/JointheBMFA/tabid/135/Default.aspx

It is fine to let children under 16 fly the quadcopter, but they MUST be under close supervision at all times. This means you should be stood next to them, ready to take over the controls without delay if an incident is looking likely. It should be reiterated that these are not toys, but serious model aircraft, with all the dangers the hobby can bring if not practiced with safety in the forefront of everything you do.

Many local authorities have byelaws about flying model aircraft in their parks, but confusingly, some only apply to IC (internal combustion engine) driven aircraft and not electrically powered versions. If you are flying in a park and a ranger or other council official tells you to stop, ask to see a copy of the regulations. Please don't knock his hat off with the 'copter, as this sets a bad tone for the rest of the discussion. If they cannot provide evidence of the local byelaws, you are within your rights to carry on flying, but it is best to land, request a copy be sent to you and then make a decision as to whether or not to fly there again, based upon the evidence provided.

The best place to fly from is a large field or car park, but with the written permission of the landowner. You may notice we have not suggested local model flying clubs, as our experience is that unless you have a model flying qualification, they tend to insist on "buddy boxes" – dual controls for new fliers and let you get in about 5 minutes flying with 3 hours of learned discourse. This is quite understandable with expensive model aircraft using conventional control systems, but ignores many of the safety benefits of quadcopters and their associated flight controls. If however, your local club has a more progressive electric helicopter section, it might be worth a try though. The BMFA has an interactive list of clubs on their website. http://clubmap.bmfa.org/ Whatever you do, please ensure you have permission to fly from your chosen site, otherwise you could be sued for trespass and any insurance may be invalid.

Soft grass is much nicer to crash land on, but a hard surface is easier for take offs and controlled landings, so a piece of chipboard about 3' square (Painted with a nice big "H" of course) makes for a good landing and take-off platform. You want to keep at least 50M away from people, dogs, houses, cars etc. so pick a spot well away from civilisation. This also means your early mistakes are not quite so public. Avoid trees, as they always win in the helicopter / tree battle. Prop guards can be a real quadcopter saver in this situation and will also prevent damage if you tip over as well.

Flying a medium lift quadcopter indoors is not recommended, unless you have access to a hanger size space, or have incredible belief in your piloting skills. The GPS positioning sensors and electronic compass will not work correctly indoors, so drifting and unexpected flyaways are a distinct possibility. Prop guards should be considered a necessity and if your radio control has the option, reduce the stick sensitivity.

First Flight

So, having followed the instructions assembling the helicopter, making sure the right prop is on the right motor (it matters, as the pairs of motors will revolve in different directions to improve flight stability) and that the battery and any other accessories are fitted correctly, it is time to think about the first flight. Hopefully you will have an experienced pilot to help you, but just in case you have not, here's a few tips.

- Pick a calm day with no more than a light breeze for your first flights. Just because the helicopter can fly in a strong wind does not mean you will be able to control it, particularly on take-off and landing.
- Turn on the transmitter first. If you have a Phantom, both sticks should be in the centre. For all other transmitters, the left – throttle stick should be all the way down.
- Connect the battery to the helicopter, keeping hands clear of the blades, just in case a motor starts up. It is worth keeping hold of the model in case it decides to start to fly away as well, if at all possible.
- Check the aircraft has fired up and that the LEDs are indicating it has acquired GPS lock and is ready to go. This may take 3-5 minutes, so be patient. You may also need to calibrate the internal compass and gyros. The manual will tell you how to do this, but it normally involves turning the helicopter slowly around in various directions.
- Once the helicopter is ready to fly, move back about 10' or so, check the area is clear of sightseers and take a deep breath, the moment of lift off is here!
- On a conventional helicopter the first stage of learning is to kind of bump around the ground a bit, gently steering the helicopter,

but able to land it quickly if it all goes wrong. With a computer controlled quadcopter, it is safer to get the thing into the air and hovering just above head height, as the high centre of gravity may cause the aircraft to tip over if it hits the ground, even at a slow speed. The electronics will also ensure a stable attitude and will help to prevent the quadcopter from flying away uncontrolled.

- Start the rotors and gently increase the throttle until the 'copter is ready to lift and a bit skittish. You then need to rapidly increase power by about another 20% or so. Do this too slowly and the 'copter might well just tip over, as it may stick slightly to the ground, then take off unevenly. A bit of a shove on the throttle will give a fast lift off, overcoming the stickiness and then a slight reduction will get the 'copter into a stable position, aiming for about 10' off the ground.
- With your new found courage, gently ease the left stick left or right, watching the helicopter rotate (yaw) gently through 360°. It may well drift with the wind while doing this, but as you have it above head height, this should not be an issue. Now with the helicopter nose away from you, use the right stick to slowly send the helicopter forwards backwards and sideways. That's it, you're flying!
- Try to fly a simple out and back route over 100' or so, to get the hang of flying nose in and nose out. On the outbound leg, the controls will be as per your controller, but on the way back, left and right will be reversed, so you need to get your brain thinking in three dimensions, as well as backwards. Don't panic if it all goes wrong and you press the wrong stick or move the wrong way. The height and space you have given yourself will give you enough recovery time to correct mistakes before they become too serious.
- If the quadcopter decides to head off on its own due to you losing orientation and pushing the stich the wrong way and it is one of the types with a return to home, now is the time to try it. Some will cause the helicopter to gain height before it flies home, while others will opt for a more direct route. Another good get out of jail card is to use the "Home Lock" feature on the DJi Phantom

and Phantom2 in Naza mode. By engaging the mode and simply pulling the right stick towards you, the quadcopter will return to you, regardless of which way it is pointing. Other designs have very similar modes available.

- Start with short simple flights and add in a few landings from time to time as well. All helicopters share the same characteristic in that they sit on a "bubble" of air about 4' in diameter. If you fly off this bubble, the helicopter will lose lift and therefore height, requiring more power. Computer controlled quadcopters compensate for this very well, with the transition to forward flight being very smooth. However, as soon as you get within this bubble - for instance descending to land, the helicopter stability is massively compromised and it could tip over or drift away unexpectedly as the air underneath becomes more turbulent. The best technique with a quadcopter is to get into a stable hover about 6' up, then ease down a few inches at a time until the landing gear is about 3" above the landing site. A positive landing is then best, pulling down the throttles quite sharply, so the bird lands and the blades stop providing any lift quickly. This should prevent any tipping over or random drifting, as the air will escape quite evenly from around the blades, making for more stable landings.
- If you are flying at high altitudes, or with a heavily laden quadcopter, you may find that any attempt at descending from height vertically causes the aircraft to become very unstable. There is a real risk of the quadcopter flipping over in its own turbulence, so you must descend in a glide slope, ideally moving the aircraft forward through the air, as if it was a conventional fixed wing machine. This is no doubt smoother, as it avoids the massively turbulent air beneath the helicopter, but takes practice not to tip the quadcopter when it lands, unless all forward motion has been arrested. In this case, fly down in a gentle slope until your are about 6' off the deck and then gently lower the quadcopter vertically to earth. Prop guards are reported to make things worse, so if you find you have stability issues, you may wish to try flying without them.

- As your confidence grows, try longer flights and more complex geometric shapes in the air. Try increasing the height to 60' or 100' and start flying further and further from your operating position. Aim for at least an hour of practice flying before moving onto to anything acrobatic or camera related. Try flying on windier days, as this makes things trickier as well.
- Keep an eye on the battery indicator and prepare to land as soon as the battery indicates it has less than 15-20% of capacity remaining or the helicopter starts to lose height.
- Once you have landed for the final time, shut the motors down, put the transmitter somewhere safe and approach the helicopter carefully. Keeping fingers away from the props, disconnect the battery and pull it out of the helicopter. Only then should you switch off the transmitter and allow spectators to come near.

Crash!!

They say that there are two certainties in life; death and taxes. If you fly any sort of model aircraft, you can add a third and that is crashing! Sooner or later, you will react incorrectly during a manoeuvre, a battery will die unexpectedly or as once happened to us, a grumpy pensioner will throw a tennis ball with surprising accuracy and force and knock your 'copter out of the skies!

Don't Panic.

Model aircraft are designed to land more heavily than you might imagine and all good suppliers keep large stocks of the main bits that break. Not a great comfort we know...

With a conventional electric helicopter, it is usual to try and shut down the motor before impact, as it lessens damage to the blades and frame, but with quadcopters, it is generally best to keep it flying and let the computer try and sort things out, even if it costs you a set of propellers. The only exception to this would be if you know you are about to hit someone – or their dog, in which case, the stopped blades will cause less damage to them, even if the damage to your quadcopter is greater.

On many designs, if things go wrong, letting go of the sticks effectively hands control back to the on-board computer and it will do its best to right things and get the helicopter back on an even keel. Failing that, fight the impulse to put in big stick movements and use small amounts of power and directional control to avoid the crash. This is where you will be ruing the decision not to fit prop guards, as it is amazing how many collisions and crashes they prevent.

If the helicopter does end up as a heap on the ground, shut off any still spinning motors and put the transmitter down, somewhere out of the way. Keeping fingers clear of the props (if there are still any attached!!), disconnect the battery and remove it. Check to see if there is any damage to the battery or if it has got excessively hot. If so, leave it where it is until it cools and then move it to a safe disposal site.

Gather up the remaining parts and take them home. It won't look so bad when spread out on the kitchen table and the machine you thought totally smashed can quite often be repaired. Plastic bodies can be cheaply replaced, with any small cracks glued or fibre-glassed, but dispose of any damaged props, as these cannot be safely repaired.

Electronics require careful checking, as the modular nature means that a fault on one board could be caused by a failure on another part of the electronics. Many retailers have an on site technician who can rebuild and test your helicopter – some for a fixed cost, while for the more handy amongst us, it may be possible to pick up a second, damaged quadcopter and make a good one out of the two.

Water damage will normally spell the end of most electronics, even if dried out thoroughly. The acidity and salinity in the water damages components and erodes the connectors. Personally, we would never attempt to put a water damaged aircraft back into service without all electronic and electrical components thoroughly tested or replaced.

Next Steps

OK, so you are now reasonably confident flying simple shapes, have crashed once or twice and can control your quadcopter in any orientation. Now is the time to start learning some advanced acrobatic techniques or most likely, fit your camera and FPV kit. Aerobatic flying is beyond the scope of this book, so we shall concentrate on aerial photography and First Person View instead.

Photography and FPV

The majority of medium lift helicopters are designed to fly with a GoPro Hero camera, but cheaper alternatives can be found and the mounts adapted to fit. Done well, aerial photography can look really quite stunning and become an immersive and absorbing hobby. First Person Viewing is equally attractive, putting you into the pilot's seat while swooping through the air, skimming rooftops and racing the 09.15 to Kings Cross... However, before we get that far, let's just look at some important information.

Reality Check

The laws around aerial photography are designed to protect privacy and ensure the safe usage of UAVs fitted with video recording equipment. There is little discrimination in law between a heavyweight commercial UAV and a smaller hobby grade unit of the type we have been discussing in this book, or more perversely, micro copters fitted with tiny "keyfob" cameras.

We estimate that about 75% of online videos posted by UK Quadcopter pilots show potentially unlawful use, possibly leading to individual prosecution and further restrictions to UAV hobby usage. A brief outline of the regulations as they stand at the moment (April 2014) is shown below.

In addition to the rules governing model aircraft use, the following further instructions apply if you are recording the camera footage. They do not all apply for FPV, where no recording takes place:

- You may not fly within 50 metres of any building, structure, vehicle, ship or person not under your direct control

- You may not fly over or within 150M of any city, town, village or built up area. (A congested area)
- You may not fly over or within 150M of any organised gathering of more than 1000 people
- You must not rely on a video downlink to control or direct the aircraft and must keep it in
sight at all times (Applies to FPV as well)
- If you are wearing video goggles – Fatshark or similar, you must have a competent observer stood next to you, visually in contact with the aircraft at all times. A child under 16 is not considered a competent observer
- You may not benefit commercially from the use of a camera equipped UAV unless qualified and insured to do so

For further clarification please refer to the relevant sections of the Air Navigation Order -
http://www.caa.co.uk/docs/33/CAP%20393%20final.pdf

To date, there has been one prosecution and one caution issued to fliers of video equipped UAVs. The prosecution was of a man who had flown a fixed wing camera equipped aircraft low over a road bridge and then over the BAE nuclear submarine base in Cumbria, while the caution was for selling footage taken from a hobby quadcopter of a school fire to a media network.

To operate commercially and to receive any exemption from any of the rules above, you must be a BNUSC rated pilot. More details here:
http://www.eurousc.com/

The height that small model aircraft with FPV systems can operate too has recently been increased to 1000', while the horizontal distance has also been increased. The requirement to keep the UAV in site however is unchanged. Spotting a white, medium lift quadcopter at 1000' is quite a challenge! We have fitted prop guards painted in a day-glow orange paint. This makes it easier to spot and tell its orientation when flying close to the maximum distance away.

Before we go any further let's look at the equipment required for both FPV and aerial photography.

FPV Requirements:

- A fixed camera, usually pointing forward and slightly down. Often this will be standard definition and mounted as close to the centre as possible. A 35mm lens equivalent will give a natural view, emulating the field of vision of the eye, although some users prefer a wider angle allowing them to see the extents of the footprint of the aircraft.
- A video downlink. As the most common video senders are located in the same 2.4GHz band as many radio controls, the slightly less congested 5.8GHz band is more popular. This avoids any potential for the video transmitter swamping the signal from the radio control transmitter and reducing the operational range. It should be noted that American regulations allow for more powerful video transmitters, so you should ensure the model you buy is legal to use in the UK. This means a power output (␣RP) of 25mw. You will often find 200 – 2000mw systems for sale in the UK, as it is not illegal to own one, just to use it. Digital and HD video link systems are now available, but the price is more than £1000 at present.
- Video receiver and monitor. There is an excellent range of monitoring systems, many with build in receivers. These range from simple LCD screens with a small non-diversity receiver Velcro'd to the back, to a set of goggles – Fat Shark is currently the system of choice, with a dual diversity receiver built in. (A diversity receiver is one with 2 or more aerials and tuners, where the receiver can choose the one with the best signal, thus providing a more stable link)
- Extra batteries – depending upon the model.
- On Screen Display Overlay – allowing flight information such as altitude and speed to be displayed in real time on the receiver.

For FPV, the lighter and smaller the equipment, the longer the flight time. Featherweight cameras may not offer the ultimate in quality, but to many the sacrifice is worth it for being able to fly longer flight times and with greater agility.

Aerial Photography Requirements

- High resolution camera, probably 12Mp still and HD video resolution and ideally with high frame rate to allow seamless low motion shots.
- Adjustable mount and ideally a motorised gimbal, to keep the camera pointing in the same direction irrespective of the movement of the quadcopter
- Video downlink & receiver – as above. This makes framing shots much easier.
- Spare control channels on the radio, so gimbal and other functions can be controlled.
- On Screen Display Overlay – allowing flight information such as altitude and speed to be displayed in real time on the video receiver. You can then almost fly the quadcopter from the screen and concentrate more on your shots.
- High Capacity batteries to run the gimbal and camera – if space and weight capacity allows.

Larger, heavy lift UAVs may also have a separate FPV camera for the pilot, with the camera operated by a second operator. This is beyond the capability of most medium lift quadcopters however.

Gimbals

It was the introduction of low cost gimbals that has really accelerated the use of cameras on quadcopters. Up until DJi introduced the Zenmuse H3 2D for GoPro Hero 3, operators had to put up with either significant movement within the shot as the quadcopter moved around, correcting for wind etc. or had to remove this motion when the video was edited, leading to loss of quality and a more restricted field of view. Full size gimbals were too heavy to be carried and cost more than the combined cost of the helicopter and GoPro combined! The latest Phantom2 craft do not even require a Gimbal Control Unit (GCU) as the control signals are derived directly from the NAZA controller, making the rig lighter and cheaper.

DJi are not however, the only manufacturer of gimbals and many cheaper models – some using radio control servos and others similar brushless motor technology are available. To date however, we have yet to find a unit that operates as efficiently as the Zenmuse, with the latest H3 3D gimbal adding a yaw correction 3rd axis, bringing the operation up to that of a fully professional gimbal, but at a fraction of the price. The downside is that these gimbals are finely balanced and tuned for specific camera models. If you upgrade the camera, you may find you need to replace the gimbal as well. It is also worth pointing out that in a crash, the gimbal is normally the first thing to suffer.

A gimbal is essentially a motorised camera pan and tilt system, but where the operator has very little input to its movements. As the aircraft tips, yaws or tilts, the Gimbal Control Unit (GCU) reacts to these change in attitude and sends commands to the gimbal to compensate. The reaction is so fast that often very little if any movement can be seen on the shot, with the end result much better than the stabilisation available on some video cameras, despite the level of movement being many times greater.

Direct drive gimbals use micro stepping motors that are essentially stalled brushless motors. This means that current consumption can be quite high, even for a lightweight GoPro camera, significantly reducing flight times. A Phantom2 fitted with a gimbal and GoPro Hero 3+ will fly for about 15 minutes, compare to around 25 minutes for a basic, out of the box model.

GoPro Cameras

As previously mentioned, the most popular camera for medium lift quadcopters is the GoPro Hero. The current model –the Hero3+ is available in three versions, White (budget), Silver (standard) and Black (Premium). Physically identical in size and very similar in weight, the cameras all offer superb quality in a robust, compact package. A little knowledge however, can help to get the best out of them. The three versions have different facilities, including different frame rates, maximum quality settings and wifi options etc. so it is worth thinking about what sort of footage you are looking to acquire and buying the right camera for the job. For just recording where you have been, the basic White model will be fine, but if you are looking to create high quality aerial photography, the better models will enable you to capture more detail and give you more options when you come to edit the footage after the flight.

- Using a high frame rate – IE 60 frames per second while recording and then playing back at 25 or 30 frames per second gives a very fluid slow motion effect. This looks particularly good on wide angle shots with a few cars or people moving around below.
- Use a lens correction effect when editing to remove the fish eye effect from the lens. This will also narrow the field of view slightly, which may help with framing or getting the quadcopter legs out of the shot.
- Turn off WiFi, as may reduce the range of the radio control system, so disable it once the camera is set up.
- In bright sunlight, the built in shutter within the camera may make action look very choppy, as the camera does not have an iris to control light and uses the shutter instead. Use a Neutral Density filter to reduce light coming into the camera for a smoother, more filmic look. Be careful not to unbalance or overstress the gimbal – if fitted though.
- If you are using the "Black" edition, use the Protune mode to gain extra detail and colour information, but remember you will need to adjust the final picture settings to get the best out of the shot.
- Use only the recommended micro SD cards, with a write speed of at least 30Mb/s. This will avoid stuttering and recording failures.

- Make sure you have the latest firmware downloaded, as there have been a few significant improvements made to the series over the past few months.

Any vibration from the motors and props of the quadcopter – or even from the control system itself, will be manifested as the infamous "Jello" shaking, where the picture appears to wobble down the screen. This is caused by the rolling or sequential shutter on the camera, which reads the information from the sensor one line at a time, starting at the top. Any lateral movement (vibration) of the camera will therefore be very visible when the shot is played back and is extremely hard to correct. Most mounts and gimbals therefore use some sort of isolation to help reduce vibration reaching the camera, but it is equally important to treat the source, by ensuring that propellers are well balanced and any motors with bent shafts replaced.

It is worth pointing out that the "Jello" effect is not unique to GoPros, but affects all cameras using a CMOS sensor. These became the standard sensor some years ago, as they offer lower power requirements, better low light capability and are cheaper to produce. Older CCD type cameras suffer less, may be too bulky or power hungry to fit to a quadcopter.

General Filming Tips

Some pilots have fitted quite large cameras to their medium lift quadcopters – up to bridge and even compact SLR size! These generally require homemade mounts and have limited video link abilities, but it just proves what can be achieved with a little ingenuity.

Once you are a competent pilot, you will find the complexity of the shots you film increases. Just as with driving a car, you will start to think much less about the basic control and much more about just where you want to position the camera platform and how the shot will develop.

Professional film makers will story board out the sequence before filming and this is a good technique to adopt. With limited flight times, you want to get the footage in the can on the first take, so a list of required shots is a good idea. Plan your shots and be prepared to shoot them out of order – if this makes more sense from a flight point of view. If a shot you had planned does not work, move on and capture the rest, maybe returning to it last – if battery life allows.

When framing photographs, use the Rule of Thirds, and position the key point of interest off centre – ideally 1/3rd of the distance from the edge of the shot and at about 2/3rd of the way up. Where the shot is a broad panorama – and let's be honest, many shots will be, think about where the horizon will fall and how the direction of sunlight will affect exposure. A beautiful shot could easily be ruined with a burnt out sky, or conversely, an under exposed landscape with the sun and sky set correctly. This may involve shooting at different times of the day to get the shot you are looking for. The still below is an excellent example of good framing and interesting use of light, even if a little more lens correction could be applied to straighten up the trees a little.

When filming public places – a ruined castle for instance, you must have permission of the landowner for the take-off site and keep at least 50M away from the building and any other visitors – unless you have permission from the site owner to film there and the site is closed to the public. With a wide angle lens, it may be difficult to judge distances through the video link, as spaces may appear greater, so make sure you keep visual contact with the quadcopter and maintain a safe height. Looking down vertically creates an interesting shot, with a gentle drift over the structure creating a continually changing vista.

Filming on hillsides creates its own challenges as the wind is less predictable. You may find that unexpected gusts can toss the aircraft around and blow you closer to trees and other obstacles than you intended! Increase your safety margin to start off with and gently close in on the target.

When shooting action shots, be aware of getting too close and putting participants in danger. Recently, there has been a case where a runner was hit by a low flying quadcopter filming an event. If this had happened in the UK, it could be in breach of the regulations, as the runner was not under the control or authority of the operator and was unaware of the close proximity of the aircraft.

Filming a friend mountain biking or skate boarding is a very different proposition. You can discuss how you intend to film the action and where the quadcopter will be positioned, ensuring any nasty surprises – like 2.5KG of quadcopter unexpectedly landing on you are significantly reduced. Make sure any spectators are kept will back, or are equally appraised of what you intend to do. If you are filming in a public area, be prepared to abort the shot and climb to a safe altitude if your filming area is compromised. Remember, you should not be closer than 50M to any person, structure or vehicle not under your direct authority. Putting up a warning sign is not sufficient.

Following the action from beside the rider is an excellent and interesting shot and tricky to master. You need to fly your quadcopter sideways, while matching the speed of the rider and keeping the shot nicely framed. Really hard to achieve but extremely satisfying when you get it right! If your quadcopter features a course lock or intelligent orientation setting, it becomes a little easier, but just be careful when you turn or pull out of the shot, as the controls may become reversed or incorrectly orientated.

Flying and shooting over water presents its own challenges. As well as the risk of landing in the drink and destroying the whole rig, wind can be unpredictable and harsher than you might think, and the sunlight much stronger. Consider a neutral density (ND) filter and add a little more height than you might do over land. We have seen more than one video where a quick push on the wrong stick has sent a quadcopter plummeting down towards the sea, not stopping and reversing as the pilot intended. Remember also that boats are much slower to respond, so avoiding a collision becomes entirely your concern. For all of this, swooping shots of yachts ploughing through the waves, or surfers catching huge waves look stunning and are worth the effort.

Filming Accidents, Emergencies and Disasters

A note about filming emergencies and disasters. If you are unlucky enough to find yourself on the scene of a fire, road accident or other newsworthy incident, please deploy your drone with care and consideration. Remember the rules about keeping 50M away from structures and people and 150m from built up areas. You should also be prepared to land if required to do so and if you see any other aircraft –IE: a police helicopter in the area. Remember also that in the UK you are not allowed to sell the footage – unless you are a licenced pilot, so think carefully about how you share the video. Pay some regard to data protection rules and don't publish personally identifiable information.

So what happens if you do annoy your grumpy neighbour? Provided you have followed the rules, you have little to worry about and to be honest, they will have little to complain about either. Even with a high definition camera, the level of detail at 50M is quite low, so it is doubtful you will have invaded their privacy. It is worth showing the footage to any upset parties, so that they can see just how distant the shots are and that you are not peering in through their bedroom window! (Unless of course you were, but in that case, you have made a rod for your own back!)

The CAA points out on their website that Data Protection rules might come into play if you store images of personally identifiable individuals or car number plates etc. Again, from 50M with a wide angle lens, it is doubtful you will capture very much, but think about how you store the footage and what shots you decide to share via YouTube and Vimeo etc.

Overflying schools and other areas where children will be playing is likely to cause offence to somebody and is best avoided to prevent bad feeling and possible confrontation. The CAA regulations prohibit flying over "Congested" areas - which means towns, villages and all built up areas. This rule alone should prevent legal pilots from ever incurring the wrath of upset residents accusing them of invading their privacy. Common sense stuff really.

Conclusion

There can be no doubt that flying quadcopters is a fun and absorbing hobby. The initial outlay can be quite high, but with careful and structured practice and conservative flight planning, there is no reason to think that you will be spending a fortune keeping your 'bird in the air.

Whether learning aerobatic maneuverers, or using your quadcopter as an aerial platform, you will find flying a continual learning curve. Basic skills might be easy to master, but the subtleties of good flying takes a lot longer.

Do consider joining a club – even if it is just an online forum. This will give you plenty of free advice – or at least opinions! Insurance is an equally good idea and you might even want to get an aviation VFR (Visual Flight Rules) map, just to make sure you do not stray into restricted airspace.

Above all, a common sense and non-confrontational approach to flying will help to reduce bad feeling towards model aircraft pilots and also to ensure the level of regulation remains reasonably low.

© Copyright 2014 Matt Jarvis

Pictures used with permission wherever possible.

About the Author:

Matt Jarvis is a keen model helicopter flier, with extensive experience flying a range of craft, from single rotor to quadcopters and beyond. He writes reviews for a number of websites on subjects as diverse as film reviews to car appraisals and contributes to various online advice forums. His day jobs have included working as a military driving instructor, producing pop concerts and directing live video shoots. He promises one day to settle down and get a proper job…

Printed in Great Britain
by Amazon.co.uk, Ltd.,
Marston Gate.